WHAT WIND WILL DO

The Miami University Press Poetry Series
General Editor: James Reiss

WHAT WIND WILL DO

Poems
by
Debra Bruce

Miami University Press
Oxford, Ohio

Library of Congress Cataloging-in-Publication Data

Bruce, Debra,
    What wind will do / Debra Bruce.
        p.   cm.
    ISBN 1-881163-18-0. – ISBN 1-881163-19-9
    I. Title.
PS3552.R7918W48 1997

811'.54 — dc20   96-29068
                                                CIP

The paper in this book meets the guidelines
for permanence and durability of the Committee
on Production Guidelines for Book Longevity
of the Council on Library Resources. ⊖

Printed in the U.S.A.

For Rick and Kevin Kinnebrew

ACKNOWLEDGMENTS

Thanks to the editors of the following magazines and anthologies in which these poems, sometimes in earlier versions, first appeared:

The American Voice: A Valediction In The Waiting Room

Articulations: The Body And Illness In Poetry (University of Iowa Press): A Valediction In The Waiting Room

Cumberland Poetry Review: A Mother's Explanations, Sobachka

The Female Body (University of Michigan Press): Beauty On The Beach

A Formal Feeling Comes: Poetry In Form By Contemporary Women (Story Line Press): The Light They Make (2 and 4)

The Formalist: Infertility, Prognosis

The Illinois Review: What Mother's Weather

Kenyon Review: Two Couples, What Wind Will Do

The Literary Review: Notes Toward A Sermon

Michigan Quarterly Review: Beauty On The Beach

New England Review: The Fitting

North American Review: Outside

Ordinary Time (The Church And The Artist Press): Difficult
Confession

Pivot: Greetings From Partyland, September Rondel

Poetry: An Argument About A Tree, Follow-Up Exam

Prairie Schooner: Desire's Recovery, I've Decided To Tell You
Anyway, Roberta, The Usual Time

Rhino: Advice From Experts

The Virginia Quarterly Review: Blessed And Brooding

The Women's Review of Books: She Promises Him

———————————

"The Light They Make" *won The Poetry Society of America's
Gustav Davidson Memorial Award.*

———————————

Thanks to Kathy Snyder for her patient help in preparing this
manuscript.

ALSO BY DEBRA BRUCE

Sudden Hunger   1987

Pure Daughter   1983

Dissolves (chapbook)   1977

CONTENTS

I.

17   A Dangerous Happiness

19   The Light They Make

21   Beauty On The Beach

23   Infertility

24   Two Couples

25   The Usual Time

26   Blessed And Brooding

27   Leopard Barrette

29   The Night Of Summerfest

30   Difficult Confession

31   I've Decided To Tell You Anyway

32   An Argument About A Tree

33   What Wind Will Do

35   Prognosis

II.

39   Greetings From Partyland

41   The Fitting

42   Desire's Recovery

43   Advice From Experts

45   Notes Toward A Sermon

46   Outside

47   A Mother's Explanations

48   Sobachka

50   She Promises Him

51   Roberta

53   A Valediction In The Waiting Room

55   What Mother's Weather

56   September Rondel

57   Kevin In Korean

59   Follow-Up Exam

I

A DANGEROUS HAPPINESS

On guard against the spring,
not trusting anything
to turn out right, I bring

such vigilance to bear
on any bud I see flared
minutely, anywhere

(on notice, myself, though all's well,
now, in all my cells)
that you, alert, can tell

it's time to stroke my back,
recite the hopeful facts
we've memorized, relax

my body with your hands.
But even in such expanding,
deepening heat, my plan's

to stay contained in case,
(no fool bloom) braced
and terse if I give praise.

At first I didn't know
if you would follow
where I had to go. The towel

I held tight around
my body I let drop down
and in the mirror found

my loss. Can a jolt
of joyous green hurt
the brown ground it bursts

through? Preposterous!
But still, between us
let's keep the boisterous

proclamations down,
agreed? Alone,
letting the shower run,

I couldn't even let you in
or show you yet, much less
let you trace the theft
of touch across my chest, to touch what's left.

THE LIGHT THEY MAKE

1

He buffs my whole body, circling each plum,
wet nipple with the tip of a plush towel,
rolls me in sun on the rug. I feel as young
as two decades back, in a backseat, learning how
to move just so and slow some gold boy down.
My body wound up tight, unwinding, was all
I wanted then, my heartbeat hard, my own,
my own. But late last winter a sudden thaw
stunned us both. Shoving our stuck storms loose,
we asked each other if.... One day I chucked
my pills, we cleared the bed, let heaped books
hit the floor—books about the clock
deep inside my body—all spring a flurry
of pages telling us hurry, hurry, hurry.

2

Deep in her seventh month, my sister dozes
afternoons, her voice still dusky on the phone
a thousand miles away. Distance sizzles
in my ear. I want to hear and I don't
want to—about the afghan she's been weaving,
her legs propped up, how new life crowds her heart,
hurts, takes her breath away, even
the crazy cravings all come true. As far
from her as I've ever been, I wait with her
and I wait alone each month. Buds squeeze
open; batches of birds hatch, this year
as always, regardless, their first notes tweezed
out high in the trees. Wisteria bulges—boom—
it blooms. My sister's son is born in June.

3

August. Couples lined up. Girls are hooked
by their belt-loops by boys as the ferris wheel
swings down, rocking, couples slowly rocked.
Locked in, we rise. I close my eyes and feel
the sky swoop through me, flown down, down.
Everybody wins.... A goldfish whips and glides
in a pouch. Wind shoves its way around.
The tent shudders as my husband pulls me inside.
But I drift away and see her waiting there—
the fortune teller—deep fuchsia hung
around her, candlelit. I won't stay with her
too long. Her eyes. My husband's voice: *What's wrong?*
He runs, grabbing my arm. But I won't
be long. He squeezes my hands: *Please don't.*

4

Wet streets, black trees, a gold leaf smacked
against our bedroom window as I smolder
beside him under a quilt made block by block
by hand by my mother's mother, getting older
than she told us, bending closer to stitch,
to tug threads tight, then tighter, worrying
she might not finish in time to watch me unlatch
her cedar chest and find it, hurrying.
Relax, my husband says, my ragged sighs
making both of us laugh. *Either way,*
we'll still be happy, right? The only light's
the bright leaves left in trees against the sky.
Of course. It's not the only thing that matters.
Come one good gust, the light they make will shatter.

Beauty on the Beach
Free Makeup Demonstration!

C'mere you handsome brute, I'll soothe your lips,
she says, and we watch his sunburned grin cool
to the mint of her circling fingertips.

Ladies, voila! His tan chest sprigged with gold,
she lets him go—long, luscious, scuffing
off in the sand. So what if I feel old

watching him disappear? Here comes a gust
to rough up the shore, ruffle my hair,
reassuring me. My hands pushed

deep in my pelvic pockets, I'm aloof
in this female flock. I stalk, sheared, sunbleached,
my bare face and supple swimmer's arms proof

I'm not like them. So why do I let her lay
me down along her chaise-longue, her bland,
handpicked example of *Before* and let her say

what she says, smiling, pointing to my cheek
where pores loom, lunar. *Horrors, ladies,*
but goodness, easy to hide! A chuckle breaks

into bits in the crowd, a rubble of shells
scrubbing my face. But now she smooths on swirls
of Ivory Bisque. A touch of concealer conceals

my laugh-lines as she tells us all, *You know,*
some ladies just let themselves get old.
Their mouth looks like a worn-out buttonhole.

Ladies, look at me. Who knows how far
I'll go? This Plain-Jane-And-Proud-Of-It
has caught a whiff of despair Sachet de Soir

can't mask, when ozone blows across the sand,
black clouds bank, the door to Sam's Fish House
slams, and a boy mutters, *Help you, Ma'am?*

but doesn't see me. Isn't it better
when he takes quick looks as I stand and hold my hips
just so, the delicate flicks of his wrist making flitter

spark in the last bits of sun over sole
and perch and cod? Ladies, what should I do
to keep him watching me go and come and go,
cleaning his hands, leaning, smiling, rubbing his rose tattoo?

INFERTILITY

Often it begins in bliss, like this:
Her husband piles the good dry wood higher
at dusk, and as the dark gets deep their fire
acquires authority. As if a wish
had been acknowledged there and must be given,
she lets the flames' heat beat against her skin,
watches their wild light. As for him,
even from himself it stays hidden—
his joy—like the next day's sun still stashed
behind the pines. Now off this couple goes
insanely early, along the beach, splashing,
talking, sleepless. She shakes a shell. He knows
that she can't wait to tell and tell. (And will.)
The bay is calm; the bell-buoys, all, are still.

Two Couples

The mother throws her voice in loops,
up high, above the baby's head,
now brings it down, it swoops and swoops;
she scoops him up and off to bed,
now comes back, flushed, famished, sits,
now bites into the buttered pulp
of artichoke. A heap of sweets
circles. She and her husband talk
of how the baby's changed their days,
how they waited. They understand
the way the other woman waits.
Last week she had her ovaries scanned.
Who knows what next? The baby's voice—
The father jumps for the bottle.
The other couple, nibbling moist,
glazed bits of apple-babka,
fix their coffee, watching them—
father humming while baby drinks.
She dumps a storm of sugar in,
stirring slowly, trying to think

that life is full, baby or not.
But summer's going, cicadas beat
their crazy song, their timbals taut.
Apples fatten in heat, in heat.
She knows they do. They deepen, drop,
sap-side smack, release their spice.
The nipple slips, the bottle plops
and rolls away, the baby cries.
He's stretched high on his father's thighs,
now dumples down again, now lies,
head hung back on his mother's knees;
looking around and around, he sees
the other couple upside-down.

The Usual Time

She pounds along in a lap-lane all her own,
roped off from the pregnant women climbing carefully
down the ladder, letting their heaviness down
to drift awhile each morning till they're due.
They see her slit the water, slipping in—
her body tapered, tight. How could they know
last month she timed her cycle, tried again,
how many times she's tried, losing time?

In the locker room she sees the others
oiling themselves; one's rubbing a mound
so small it hardly shows but she's a mother
already and knows her girl rides high inside.
One says her five-month stupor's lifted, left
her feeling smug at six. Punchy with pleasure
she swears last week her pastor intoned, text
laid open, *When God created the uterus....*

Over there, the trim, dry lap-swimmer slides
into sweats. Once, believing she'd conceived,
she felt her dreams deepen and saw, one night,
her grandmother who'd come back to help her find
a rum-soaked fruitcake hidden in the hutch
beside the rocker. She locks her locker and goes

back home, trying not to make too much
of things. But now spring is at it again:
the plum puts out shoots, twig-spines, and sometimes
the rocker seems to mock her as it rocks her.

BLESSED AND BROODING

The months ahead look like huge, cluttered rooms
I want to kick my way across and get
to you. But you're just barely there. And women
have a knack for this, I'm told. So I wait
and wait. Your father knocks on wood—on the carved,
curved arm of the walnut rocker he hauled
upstairs for me two summers ago, before
we knew how many times we'd try and fail,
try and lose. Now nothing seems sure
except that cicadas' shrill cries rise
all day, then slow to static, then scrape our screens
at dusk. When will they stop? I want the crazed
fall winds to come, come down and crush the sky
to bright bits, then strip it bare. But the sun
stays high so long this one last summer
before your birth. (I'll knock on the rocker again.)

In our cellar there's cider in heavy jugs
to mull and drink from handmade mugs on days
the color of dull knives, before you come.
While I rock, rock and talk, and your father walks
around the edge of the braided rug.

LEOPARD BARRETTE

Your crumpled message shot across the floor
to my sandal-toe. Reaching down dusky hose
I finally had permission to wear,
I slid the note across my lap, unnoticed
by our newly married teacher, Mrs. Day,
and slowly unfolded the unambiguous sketch
you'd made of our teacher as she lay—
Miss Sobiski No More! the title read—
about to be transformed by Mr. Day,
arranged above her, as improbably endowed
as any man imagined by sixth-grade girls
who still looped arms at recess, giddy,
and reached across each other's backs to twirl
a twist of hair or give a stinging snap
to a strap on a first bra, de rigueur,

suddenly, that spring. The boys who packed
the playground were crew-cut, cool, ignoring us.
In hazy heat I let my hair hang back,
and waited for your caress—busy, criss-cross—
your concentration snug against my nape,
the braid tugged tight. One day a shout, *Lesbos!*
shot up as high as a ball that seems to escape
all the scrambling players down below,
scattered the boys and made us make a space
between us in the grass so the world would know
what we were not. But the word spread
through June, and in the field we cut across
between our houses, summer horses turned
to a groom's touch, their coats brushed down
and down, their tails tucked up. They were returned

each day at noon, checked for flecks of hurt,
their every undulation trained to win.
That fall by our homeroom door the boys were waiting
to cluck their taunt, but then we joined them,
and everyone forgot. And as for the gift
you gave me much later, your hand-painted
leopard barrette, who would have noticed
how long we leaned together while you arranged
my hair within its clasp? We were out of danger
by then, my own commotion making no sound,
unlocked lockers clanging all around.

The Night of Summerfest

I told you everything, relived my shame.
Admitting blame, I'd breathe again, I thought.
I tried to calmly call it by its name,
as if to talk could tame what's talked about.

Beneath his mobile whose moons and planets, touched
by subtle currents all night long, would change
above his bed, our son slept on throughout.
I told you everything, relived my shame.

That day we'd watched trained, belted boys whose aimed,
high kicks broke boards but did not hurt
their bare feet or their master's hands.
Admitting blame, I'd breathe again, I thought.

Our son cried when grown women rose to shout
at the sky and stomp, their brass gongs banging
until the ground was pounding where we sat.
I tried to calmly call it by its name,

telling him they danced that way so rain
would make things grow. I promised him they'd stop
because he begged me to. I tried to explain,
as if to talk could tame what's talked about.

Back home we scooped him sleeping from the car
and tiptoed quickly to his room, arranged
his nest of pillows, bears, and left him there.
Whose summer has been maimed.
I told you.

Difficult Confession

At four o'clock I lock the church and leave.
I've got to clear my head. The heat of this slow,
smoky fall hangs on, won't let me go.
I know I failed her. I told her to receive
His light as a guide and do what she believed
was right. That's not what she wanted. No.
I listened to her breathe, the sweat below
my hairline prickling, twisting my heavy sleeves.
I watched her go. Behind the rectory
the apple trees are dragging on the ground.
If I hear her voice, if He sends her back to me....
This thick sky holds me back. I want it gashed
by sun, the smell of apples coming down,
splitting open, smashed.

I'VE DECIDED TO TELL YOU ANYWAY

But first I have to find the perfect spot.
I balance, rock to rock, looking back
at you, although at sixty-nine you're still
limber enough to climb down to a lake
you've never seen, led by a daughter out
on a ledge; you scan the sky, step back, back,
and finally arrange yourself in sun.
Where do I begin? And what if all
you say is *Chin up, doll, it's over now*
while speedboats rip by, whip around, buck
their wake? Will you listen? Some nights, still,
I wait till daylight for a few scraps
of sleep.... I watch you watch a windsurfer's one
wing drop in a lake that's aching cold.
How well I know the lesson: Look, she's up,
she glides again. You pat your shirt for a smoke
which means it's time for me to speak. Once,

you tried to teach me how to ride the surf.
I swam all day, but wave after wave slammed
me down on my lungs. We sit here now as waves
smash toward us–steep, deep green-black, manic–the panic
is mine, all mine.

An Argument About A Tree

She's never had a garden in her life,
this daughter here, but thinks she knows enough
about trees to tell him it's an elm.
He knows it's not an elm. The trunk's not rough
enough, he tells her, tugging at a lip
of bark, then stepping back to scan the crown.
Listen—he knows his trees, and flowers too.
Back home he had to cut his sick elms down
one spring, the spring his pin-oak bulged and broke
the bench he'd made to circle it. Their rosebush—
only he knew how far back to trim,
or how long one low rose would take to push
open. They walk the six blocks back, heat
from concrete rising around her high-rise
and cicadas grinding their whines higher,
higher. He doesn't like to criticize
his children's lives. No matter where they go
he'll always visit and only once left,
still bitter, under a white summer sky.
It's better just to keep things to yourself.

A bright book hits the table with a slap—
Trees Of The World. After she leaves for work
he closes his eyes, trying to see the tree.
Maybe he'd better have another look,
he thinks, carrying the book six blocks back
to where they stood a little while ago.
It's an elm. The words crawl up into his chest.
Ulmus. Elm. Why didn't he know?
He hears his heart, he feels himself skid down
a steep slope. No. He's on level ground.
He's here, on a city's grid where daughters glide
along macadam in their compact cars.
He spreads his hands out on the furrowed bark.

WHAT WIND WILL DO

I
My father knows what wind will do.
He swears he never knew before.
He never dreamed one gust could break
his hundred-year-old oak in two.
Until a sound like gunshots shocked
him awake late one August night,
sweat-soaked, almost seventy.
Somehow he knew it was his oak
but went downstairs to check the doors,
in case, then turned the porch-light on.
He saw, in the rain's blown, blinding sheen,
his old dog, Bandit, scared of storms.
He thought of calling, but what's to say?
He loosened Bandit's clump of chain.
He says he thought of us, his kids,
all six, asleep, in different states.
(My father's yard is dense and black
on summer nights, an acre deep.
The porch-light never reached that far.
You'd have to feel your way out back.)
Toward dawn he was still sitting there,
big baggy Bandit in his lap.
He says he felt ridiculous.
He heard a siren whip the air.
Trees down all over town, he heard,
the radio turned on, then saw
what wind will do, the damage done,
when morning let some wet light through.

II
My sister slips by, smirking, pokes my hip,
You think he's getting senile? No, not yet.
He walks in circles with his coffee cup,
tells us again how he watched one last branch
loosen, let go. Bare sky showed. *Nothing
we can do. Only the tree really knows.*
Aunt Grace hoots—as if a tree could think!
She's always known he had a few screws loose.
(As if a tree could feel the days grow long,
her brothers pitching horseshoes in its shade,
their voices looping low along the lawn.)
Grace glares and turns her back; her walker whacks
and whacks, like lawnchairs being stacked. The oak
can't hear a thing. Her brothers are all gone

except my father, whose smoker's lungfilled laugh
sends her sputtering, clumping back and forth.
Ridiculous! (As if the oak could know
that one last year its leaves would dull down, fall
and circle, berserk, above the crusted snow.)

Prognosis

I hold my breath and balance on a cliff,
instructed not to focus on the edge.
Instead of *when,* my sentence starts with *if,*

though surreptitiously I spot a cleft
of rock and tiptoe toward the hope I can wedge
myself inside, be safe upon this cliff.

But what I'm searching for is what I've left
behind—the snug, sunlit privilege
of making plans with *when* instead of *if.*

Some climb the years, and in their sixty-fifth,
join Tuesday's book-club, take a course in French,
while others, younger, balance on a cliff

listening for news whose wild relief
allows them one more step, one increment
of *now,* not *then.* My sentence starts with *if*

and plummets easily—if one streaked leaf
descends to circle at my feet, I clench—
hold my breath, balance on this cliff
where everything I think begins with *if.*

II

GREETINGS FROM PARTYLAND

In number 3, the Birthday Girl turns 4.
We don't have time to memorize each name.
Whoever she is, the bright striped birthday chair
announces to her 20 preschool friends

and us, too rushed to memorize each name,
that she's the one whose life we celebrate.
Each party room has someone's 20 friends,
all celebrating simultaneously,

but she's the one whose life we celebrate
in 3 at 1:15, and you, the mom,
are celebrated simultaneously;
your gift is to relax and watch your child

from 1:15 till 2. Yes you, the mom,
so many things to do, allow yourself
this gift—sit back, relax, and watch your child,
and if you find yourself remembering

the things you meant to do, allow yourself
to let them go—here comes our sculpted cake.
And if you find yourself remembering
some sloping creamy cake your mother baked....

just let it go—here comes our sculpted cake.
A commotion of sugar shaken into her mixing bowl,
the sloping, creamy cakes *your* mother baked....
But no one misses what they never knew—

a commotion of sugar shaken into a mixing bowl?
Snap out of it! We're here to simplify,

and no one misses what they never knew.
The child who slowly struggles with a gift

snaps out of it as our scissors simplify
to snips the bow too complex to untie
for this child who slowly struggles with the gift
of concentration's rapture which we must

snip, like a bow too complex to untie.
We keep them moving, let no child disappear
in concentration's rapture. Now we must,
for 30 minutes in our climbing room,

keep them moving, let no child disappear
in the mix of 40 kids who flash by, flushed,
for 30 minutes in our climbing room.
Children you know, children you've never seen

all mixed up, 40 kids who flash by, flushed.
Don't forget to camcord—there they go,
the children you know. Children you've never seen
will reappear on your home-video.

Don't forget to camcord—there she goes.
Why not make next year's reservation now?
Your child will reappear on video.
It goes so fast! So why not beat the rush

by making next year's reservation now
for whoever she was, in the bright striped birthday chair,
who goes so fast...so why not beat the rush!
In number 3, a Birthday Girl turns 4.

THE FITTING

He smells like leather and mint and the El that shot
him through the city. Now he slips
his headstrap off, his black patch. But not

for them—the ones who heaved at him and swung
their taunt: *Let's see what's under there.*
The ocularist looked at him so long,

so long the last time he was here, she knew
what hazy brown to brush the iris
in her hand, amber flashing through.

Around the pupil she touched in cinnamon.
Now she lifts his chin, opens
his damp lids, like lips, to tuck it in,

nudges the mirror toward him, smiling: *there.*
The headstrap's left its track
above his temples in his blue-black hair.

He looks at himself. She waits. *Looks alright.*
he says, rubbing his neck, his jaw,
turning, touching his earring, a bud of light.

Desire's Recovery

Even a touch seemed almost blasphemous
for many months, even my husband's hands,
until one night he crushed the curtain open
to join me uninvited in the shower,
his slowly soaping strokes reminding me,

convincingly, I still had curves. We made
the surgeon's words begin to fade, as stitch
by stitch my skin was getting back its silk,
although from nipple down, one contour's round
would never be the same. I'd never lean

so languorously I might forget, though late
light on a brick wall releasing all
its daylong stored up sun might still warm
my back and make me want to wait, as if
the one whose gold chain sparked against his chest

might meet me there again and take me back
to where the only danger was his hands
so busily and easily unstrapping
my backless blouse, my skin etched with that summer's
mesh of matted twigs, weeds. Now just

one gust of this year's full-blown June across
the bed alerts me like something I forgot
to say, then makes me hesitate—the word
future's fragile,
voluptuous vowels like something I might reach

to touch and touching, burst.

Advice From Experts

As if at my request a funnel cloud
might change its path or gyrate carefully
between two houses, not breaking anything,
most books on motherhood prescribe a *firm
but friendly way to redirect* the urge
that surges through my thirty-pounder, hurtles
him pounding on the floor. He must be taught
the taut ways of adults. But spare the rod,
they say. And so I hold him gently headlocked
in my lap, restraining both of us.
Tornado weather's here; by now I know
the story of the Kansas children whose mother
led them down below then climbed back up,
whose brave and shaky camcorded horror
shows up on all three spring tornado shows.
Through three raw weeks of rain the rivers rise
and rise. My dreams are roiling—there's Nicky Jax
whose mother called the cops or said she called.
Below his porch we crowded in crawl-space
to watch this bad kid *get it*. The bottle
he pitched toward rocks inches from where we flinched,
waiting, just missed. And still we heard
his whimper as he walked above our heads.

A sudden stunning sun, but behind it's
violence—the weathermen have warned.
My son is peering into a peony,
then shakes its shag, then gags it till the whole
flower flumps. I wish I hadn't seen
my neighbor watching; she points to her one
and only grown son, jobless, come

back home, who lifts a listless hand to greet
my stare: *Now that one there, he wouldn't mind,*
he wore me out, who spends these stormy spring
days on a daybed pushed against a wall.
It's possible—isn't it?—that she longed
for him three decades back as I longed
so long I lost track and wouldn't look
at greensick skies gone black and didn't care
how hard hail hit or what it hurt. This year

on rare May days I rock my son and rocking,
slow my pulse and lull him slowly back,
down, heavy in my lap. Come June,
in stupefying heat I'll mourn my way
through mounds of clothes he's twisted out of once
and for all. The rest as usual—
our apple tree will fill with fruit too fast
for anyone to eat, then lose it—
an abundant, busted ooze will soak the grass, then dry.

Notes Toward A Sermon

Early spring. But if I speak too soon
of what I've seen just watching from my room—
the tulip magnolia's bloom blown away—
if I speak this way of holding onto faith,
who will listen to me, Who will come back?

They say they don't need Him anymore. Sun
on the backs of their necks as they run
all April, hearts beating down to their heels—
they tell me now they believe in what's real,
that there's no going back.

Thinking of them, I pace in loose, mown grass
whose fragrance follows me all the way to Mass
this Easter day. A crowd of them inside—
and my one chance to help Him live who hides
from them all year, right here, to bring Him back.

I walked in a wheatfield once, held a dry
sunlit seed in my hand. It couldn't die,
couldn't grow. It was tight, shut, shellacked.
How can I tell them how hard it was to crack
my own heart open and bring myself back?

Before I speak I'll press the fresh-cut branch
of evergreen down until it's drenched
in water I blessed myself and wave it here,
there, fling nets of moisture on their hair,
wet their cheeks. They'll cross themselves. He's there.
I pray they know it. All I can do is that.

Outside

I warned him not to touch, but my son thumbed
a thorn anyway, opened his hand and rubbed
up to the topmost bud. *It doesn't hurt!*
Feel it! What should have brought pain was soft
as brush-tip to my touch. Spring's mixed up.
That's why I'd spent the morning on my knees,
according to instructions from a friend
of a friend, to cut the roses that froze back
to the first five-leafed brackets and hope
for bloom. My son held up a stick to swing
a stringy worm. Neither of us heard
our neighbor coming up the walk to watch,
scatter chit-chat, and then, matter-of-fact,
her questions: *Will you adopt another one?*
Couldn't you have any of your own?

The other day I stroked the first few wisps
of down on his shin. How many times since then
he's hoisted up a pantleg to proclaim
to anyone, *Look! Hair on my legs!*
I'm going to be a man! After she left
I held him hard, smelled the not quite sweet
sweat on his scalp, behind his ears, his neck.
And that was that. At our backs, the sun
kept making its subtle moves across the lawn.

A Mother's Explanations

for Kevin Lee

The crossing guard high-fives the red-haired boy,
slides back in place the backpack that's about
to be sloughed off a smaller boy, then swats
the swinging tassels on both blond twins' hats
until they shrug and laugh. Now noticing
this woman's child he's learned to recognize,
the guard stares down as if he's focusing
on some elusive, complicated thought—
the boy's black bangs, the unmistakable eyes—
which look away until there's no place left
to look but at the crossing guard, whose look,
which will not stop, is more than *looking,* yet
the boy's too young to say exactly what.

Last night, his night-light on, his questions pressed
against his mother, he made his room zoom
with what he wants to know—the names of moons
not ours, the sun going down not *going*
but withholding while we roll and wait to ride
across its light. He lets her only
tell him certain stories now, has banned
from her lips all songs which he insists he's grown
beyond, though she's allowed to unravel
a riddle he got from kids at school, and lie
with him until he sleeps and the dark ladles
up its stars in shapes he's memorized
from glowing stickers stuck above his bed.

But come the day, today, let his mother be
beside him, waiting at the curb; when she sees
the way this crossing guard regards her son,
what words will help her to articulate,
to speculate about a grown man's
who-knows-what—his losses, hurts—
whose hand, held up, can make it safe to cross?

SOBACHKA

Not wanting to offend, Yelena waits
until her boy gets out of hand and then,
apologizing first—*so rude to speak
my Russian with American friends*—unravels
a rapid skein of reprimands until
it's wrapped around her Sasha in her lap.
My son, still in the sandbox, listens, *That's
from another country, Mom.* But never mind
countries. When Sasha slides back into the sand
they dig down hard, discussing as they go,
the trip they'll make to Jupiter's Red Spot,
how they'll build their rocket ship. Never mind

their mothers down below, one searching
through her phrase-book in the sun from word
to word as the other tries to tell her where
their boys have flown. The preschool wall is splashed
with brilliant-colored countries where each child
was born, and the kids' tongues take to the tang
of language as they gobble up each other's
homemade latkes, spring rolls, chap chae.
But some afternoons a mother might hesitate,
puzzled by the teacher's talk, waiting
for her child to see her there and come, collide
into her thighs, laughing, then quiet down
and translate up to her. If my face aches,
so must Yelena's, stretching to express,
our gestures sketching, revising. Suddenly
a dog barks—Sasha yelps, *Sobachka!*
My son repeats, *Sobachka!* She explains,
little dog, but I, too, like *sobachka*

and say it back to her and see her pleasure,
intense and obvious, as if we'd tasted
the first warm, torn off pieces of challah
at Shabbat. Now both boys bolt

to chase the dog along the chain-link fence
and even after he's gone they bat the word
between them, *Sobachka!,* running, hooting, as if
they'll never stop, then suddenly spotting something else to do,
they let it drop.

She Promises Him

I'll never see her again in her snug,
flannel-soft jeans, her thick black hair tied back.
She fed me all summer long. She cracked
bad jokes as she opened avocados, tugged
the nut loose—there—its silky flesh for me.
Two women in a house, their menses come
together. I don't know why. Warm rum,
swirled with butter, eased us slowly to sleep.
But I won't see her again, smell the breeze
with its sweet stink of low-tide, hear the lap,
lap of water coming back. She got brown,
sleek, oiling her shoulders, belly, knees.
Another life—slippery rocks slapped.
The sun came pounding, pounding its glitter down.

ROBERTA

Spinning records on my fingertips
is how I'd spent my thirteenth spring until
Roberta climbed my father's oak, straddled
and lightly bounced the branch above my head,
then said what she said.... Through every song I'd closed
my eyes, hummed, and bit my bottom lip.
But no song spoke of this. Didn't she know
that sleek-haired Larry the bagboy was my love,
whose grocery baskets clashed, clung, as he leaned
to line them up and herd them back inside
the A&P? Hadn't I clawed through velvet

curtains, crawled backstage illicitly,
clamped my legs around a rockstar's waist
until two cops tossed me into a heap
of weeping boppers just like me? The leaves
she shook made a whoosh I wished would shush her words.
The whack on blacktop of my brother's ball
stopped; above his head, around and around
it rolled before it finally swaggled down
into his hands. He didn't look our way.

My bedroom door, which had no lock, stayed shut,
and no one knocked. What I remember's not
just her complicated mouth, but fear
that rode my body like a rod straight
down to the floorboards where we stood. A glance
was all my mother gave as we emerged,
though soon she'd waylay me, one sticky night
after Larry wooed me with his grip
on the oak's harsh bark, his chinups high.

He grunted joyously, then hit the ground.
He left his handprints on my halter-top.

The ocean that swayed inside me as I lay
against Roberta on a cot, dazed
with sunburn on her parents' cottage porch
that summer, would subside. And what I miss
is not Roberta, really, but her pleasure's
pressure, my body ready, rowdy, the years
since then of resolution and permission's
rush. No one prodded us apart.
We rose, clear-headed, heading into fall.

A VALEDICTION IN THE WAITING ROOM

Never in that summer of my first
muscular kiss, my chin rubbed rough
by his, as I stumbled past the kitchen's
tiny night-light to my room to roll
in pleasure all my own, would I have dreamed
of this. Although my Aunt Irene prayed
and prayed for children, none came. But what
did I know of that? She slid back on the slats
of an Adirondack chair, her eyes half-closed,
while my sisters and I swam and dripped and hopped
on hot feet around her on the beach.
It's almost summer now, but here I sit—

a washout in fluorescent light, joined
by my husband, whose hair, when combed just so
across his crown, can make a hopeful ghost
at most. *Childless,* my Aunt Irene. But now
child-free is the phrase whose high gloss denies
loss, yet if savored long enough
releases its essence of restless emptiness.
Oh women! Remember the long, bare beach
just barely lit, just you and him and the dog
you'd loved almost a decade long damp
and happy? Now I can't count the times
I've watched my husband hold up tiny vials
in white light, squeeze the dropper, watch
his watch, then let the tremulous drop drop
as we held our breath.... Certain words are not
spoken here. Her hands on my belly, her face
turned from mine, the doctor pressed my uterus
as if to seal a stubborn envelope,

pronounced me *healed, contracted, closed.* Although
they were a thousand miles away, I know
my sisters sat together and know what words
tumbled onto the table between them, *lost
the baby,* the kitchen windows wild with snow
speeding up, coming down. By spring

it was time to try again. Again I tried
and tried and tried, like a manic comic
who slams herself against a wall, slams
and falls. Sometimes when this room's crammed
with silence and one more couple's coming
through the door, I'm edgy as a car-alarm,
about to yelp—*too late! too late!* But who
will listen? Not women who fly from three
adjacent states to see this specialist,
sun scanning each plane as it circles
in the air. Like me, like us, they know
about the clock that ticks, tolls, the river
that rolls below the hills behind the houses
where we lived as girls. What would I say
to my mother if she came banging at this door,
What's taking you so long? who bloomed and bore
six times in seven years? Or Aunt Irene,
still saying her rosary, praying down
to the bud of His body for my ovaries,
uterus? Or to the one I was,
still leggy, high-hipped, who still had time to slip
off into summer streets where boys, stripped
to the waist, leaned against gleaming cars and swapped
the details of fantastic accidents.

WHAT MOTHER'S WEATHER

At *Toys R Us* a woman spatters slaps
across her toddler's cheeks until he sinks
down in the basket, whimpering. My son
is on my hip, calm, but I feel her rough
relief. Her basket bucks across the lot.
Maybe she's lurched from need to need, no break
in sight from the boy she buckles down, hard,
before she drives away. I tell myself
*I'd never lay a hand...*instead I've spread
my rage from room to room and let my son
trail me, pleading, until the whole house
hurt. I know by now he knows the sound
unspeakables, spoken, make.

What mother's weather's too wild? Whose child is safe?
Sometimes I've let him rescue me. Just two,
his reassuring monosyllables
already memorized, his steps insistent,
circumspect, circling me where I sit
dumped on the playroom rug. When he pats
my hair, the horror of every error pours
over me; what harm I've done, done,
he shoves into my arms.

SEPTEMBER RONDEL

I watch you go. But suddenly you storm
out of line, rush back to me, your breathing warm
against my neck as I lift you, return
with you to her to whom you now must turn
in your distress. That's what you have to do.
I watch you go,

then with the other mothers disappear.
Back home, as if on cue, I note this year's
one sunflower—as if by rote it shot
its flares out high above your head, but
it now surveys the ground—or seems to.
I watched you go.

KEVIN IN KOREAN

My sizzling son, who's almost six,
who loves to talk and hates to sit,
makes such a sudden, steep descent
into silence that I pretend
to casually walk by. I look
for trouble but it's just his book
about the country where he was born,
open to his favorite story:
a tiger tears in torrid rage
down a mountain, across the page,
toward a village in which a woman
feeds her child sweet, dried persimmon
to calm its cries. My son knows well
a story he can tell himself
how once upon a time I yearned
but had no child and had to search
and search for him, and then to fly,
to carry him across the sky.

Has he even heard me yet?
Now he turns to the alphabet
in Hangul where one long, gray day
we lay on the rug and made our way
from sound to corresponding sound
when suddenly as if he'd found
his balance on a balance beam
he pushed my hand off, grabbed his pen
and spelled his own name, so absorbed
he wasn't with me anymore.
And now he's practicing again,
ignoring me even as I bend

so close I know he knows I'm there.
I touch his prickly summer hair.
I rub his neck and lean down close
as he keeps writing, as he goes,
resolving, not dissolving loss,
who must return because he must.

Follow-Up Exam

Only when I lift both arms above
my head, as when a child is asked *How big?*
and reaches high and solemnly and waits
to be released by whoops of praise; and only

since that long girlhood of mine is long
gone, my hospital gown open, as I hold
this pose at your request so your hand can guide
their gaze across my breasts; and even then

only these discerning interns would notice
my subtle loss of shape, last summer's scar.
As far as anyone can tell, the wish
my well-wishers had for me to push beyond

the unspeakable news you gave one year ago
is granted. They call my name each time I turn
to look away as if I'd heard a voice
behind a screen at dusk. I must return

to you each season, to your hands' brisk passage
across my flesh, each nipple rubbed for no one's
pleasure, in pure thought, and finally,
your findings. I make my well-trained terror wait

for you to give permission not yours to give
which I grab from you each time you shake my hand
and let me go. As far as anyone knows,
even you, we'll meet again when pears are long

since fallen, soft, scuffed. I'm off
for now. I'm on my feet, outside, out there
where all the others seem to be, where another
brazen summer noon is holding forth.

Debra Bruce is originally from Albany, New York and was educated at the University of Massachusetts, Brown University, and the Iowa Writers' Workshop. She is the author of two previous collections of poetry, *Pure Daughter* and *Sudden Hunger*, both published by the University of Arkansas Press. She is Associate Professor of English at Northeastern Illinois University and lives in Chicago with her husband, Rick Kinnebrew, and their son Kevin.